THE FORSAKEN MUSE, A WOMAN'S JOURNEY FROM SORROW TO HOPE

A book of poetry with images about a woman's quest for beauty, love and her own destiny.

Rowena Isidro

AuthorHouse™ UK Ltd.
500 Avebury Boulevard
Central Milton Keynes, MK9 2BE
www.authorhouse.co.uk
Phone: 08001974150

First published by AuthorHouse   04/11/2011

ISBN: 978-1-4567-7789-0

This book is printed on acid-free paper.

Because of the dynamic nature of the Internet, any web addresses or links contained in this book may have changed since publication and may no longer be valid. The views expressed in this work are solely those of the author and do not necessarily reflect the views of the publisher, and the publisher hereby disclaims any responsibility for them.

authorHOUSE®

Dedicated to forgotten muses all over the world that were once upon a time the inspiration of great creativity, to the 'Divine Hand' who guides me, to my lovely girlfriends, my wonderful family & other friends who never lost faith that I can do this. ♥ ♥ ♥

My own muses.

Poetry is the language of the soul.

Foreword

This book started from a personal interest to find a book of poetry with images a year ago. I have always loved writing as well as reading poetry ever since I was little, but I wanted to read them with some pictures to look at. I searched for one without success, and so thought about doing it myself. This coincided with a developing interest in photography, and collaboration with photoartists where we started to produce some beautiful images. The rest is history.

My need aside, I have always been passionate about women's issues and what I can do to help. Every woman has her own story of going through challenges and pain. There is a *Forsaken Muse* in all of us that needs attention, healing and support. I can identify with it, and I have spoken to so many women who said it resonates with them.

The book goes through a journey from despair to awakening, healing and triumph at the end. The poems in Volume I called *'Songs of Lamentation, My Life is Out of Rhyme'* can be quite painful to read for some, but I wanted to show the realities of life so we can appreciate when we have been through them. Volume II, *'I Endure, I Suffer, I Give Birth'* takes us further to the woman's journey where she starts to awaken to her natural ability to fight for survival, to do something to change her situation, where she suffers and yet she is involved in birthing something beautiful within her life. Volume III, *'Changing…Loving myself, Loving others… Finding my destiny'* shows us the beauty of her transformation, where she now has confidence to move forward, reconciles herself with herself, understands who she really is, and eventually, starts to think beyond herself to help others. Volume V, *'The Forsaken Muse Finds Herself'*, summarizes this new awareness, the new consciousness that every woman needs to have to establish her place in society.

Just like most women, I'm going through my own personal journey. I am not immune. This book has not been so easy to write. I was surprised at the intensity of my feelings whilst writing. Very painfully, I went through the turmoil, the travail and eventual triumph at the end that my muse in the story went through as I was writing it. We can say it is poetry, but life imitates art, the same way art imitates life. The two, life and art, are intrinsically linked to each other. I thought this was only a story I was writing, but I went through a lot of the emotions in the story which transported me through various years of challenges and upheavals in my life. Some of my material was written from long ago, and some of them fairly recent.

And this is why I strongly support women bonding together whether through book reading, spa workshops, get-togethers, dancing, seminars or any activity where all can learn from one another, and where those who are stronger (which is a subjective term I admit), can support those who are weaker at different periods of time. There is strength in unity, as with everything else. Just knowing we are not alone can help to lighten the load. (Please refer to *Further Information* at the back of this book to access support and other materials for women).

A few weeks ago, whilst writing, and in this mode of self-discovery, I went away to the islands to think and 'feel' about life, and contemplate on where I was and where I wanted to be. If I were to look at myself a few months back, I would not have recognized myself. I will be able to squeeze out a few tears, that much I can say, but the self-examination won't last for long. There is a change that has happened, and is still happening within me. It's not complete, of course, I am still 'work in progress' but I have started. This is what I tell myself, if you look at my poetry in Volume III called *'Changing'*:

I am a woman in a hurry,
Life is too short to think a lot about myself…
It is not about me, it is not about me.
…..That is my most important change.

And by the way, to men who understand, you are welcome to join us in this journey of self-discovery. We know you also have your own challenges, where there might be differences, but there are also similarities. And so to all my dear kindred spirits, may you find your own 'truth' as you witness the Forsaken Woman's journey through poetry.

This book is for women, and therefore also for men.

Let me take you on a journey
Beyond the pain
Beyond the sorrow
There's a story to be told
        a woman's life,
        a woman's truth
        waiting to birth,
        so full of promise,
        so full of hope.

Songs of Lamentation
...my life is out of rhyme...

Volume I

The Forsaken Muse

I am sorry
I can't give you
beautiful images anymore.
My eyes are downcast
There's no emotion to draw
My wrinkles show.
But let's take one last photograph
Try to squeeze the last smile from me,
the last ounce of life from my weak body.
Once more with feeling,
I will smile,
I promise
you won't see the tears
falling from my eyes.

No Feeling

No feeling
Nothing
Numb
A worm.
That's what you think I am.
I deserve to feel,
To be loved,
To live again.
I will.

The Show is Over

Let me take one last look at my stage, my famous world,
I owned it then, every clap from the crowd,
Every standing ovation, every admiring shout.
The show is over, it has been for awhile
It is all so quiet and dark,
Not a shadow in sight except for one soul
Looking at the mirror tonight.
I searched around and tried to sing, the echo coming back to me,
I moved to dance with aching bones, I could hardly take a turn.

Who is this woman, familiar old lady?
She must understand, like her, I'm lonely,
I looked at the mirror again and again,
I asked out aloud 'Who is she?'
There was no answer, and then I discovered,
That one lonely soul was really me.

Kiss

You
never
knew
then,
but
every
look
you
gave
me
was
a
kiss
to
my
aching
soul.

Paper Boats

Paper boats sail on rainy nights
Like childhood dreams.

Come Before Winter My Darling

I met you in summer
When days were long and warm
Autumn has come,
Just as you were gone.
Most leaves have turned brown
There's a few more leaves to fall,
Come before winter my darling
And make me feel warm.
........I'm still waiting.

Backstreet Love

(A Honky Tonk Girl's Song)

I love in darkness where no one can see
Where my only witness is a deserted alley.
I wait patiently for you to appear
Not knowing how long it will be.
One moment of joy
After days of sorrow,
It is a cycle....
Maybe today, maybe tomorrow.
I see your shadow approaching
My heart beats faster,
I agonize and travail....
Every tear shed drives my pain away,
I curse the futility of it.
Let me ask you my sweetheart-
How long can we make this backstreet love last?

Tragic Love
(a Haiku)

You are hers,
me his
While we think
of you and me
Tragic love
we have.

Your Hand's Warmth

I miss the touch of warm hands
That give me a sense of 'home'
I hardly see them now, even
Have they gone cold?

Some Dreams Will Never Rhyme

There are dreams that remain by the wayside,
Discarded, abandoned,
set aside and forgotten,
They're like poetry that never rhyme.
We keep on waiting….
searching for the perfect timing,
smooth words, rhythm and lines
Only to realize the poem never comes.
Your eyes will never lie,
I see no love as I look at you
I wait for the rhyme as time flies
Alas, the world is passing by.
Somehow tonight, I remember our dreams,
But all those dreams are gone now.
I cannot pretend to be like a child
building fragile imaginations in my mind.
There is no hope to draw from,
I can't dream dreams anymore.
They're like tangled, unresolved rhymes…
Yes,
    unfinished poetry.

I Tried Calling You Today

I tried to call you today
to find out how you were…
But your phone was busy…..
would have wanted to talk,
so badly.
Then the desire died down
after awhile…...
would have wanted to know
how you were,
since we saw each other….
anyway…...
maybe I'll try again,
another day.
But I miss you.

I Was Waiting to See You

I waited outside to see you
Wanted to hear your voice
Feel your touch
Talk to you
See you smile
Just one last time.
But the gate was closed
The door was locked
There was no answer inside.
I waited a minute, an hour, a day
'Til hope faded in the evening.
I was not welcome,
There was no room for an unwanted visitor.

Love is the Dying Sun

Love is like the dying sun in the late afternoon,
seeping through the crevices of old abandoned doors.
It crawls and struggles trying to keep alive,
the light flickering on and off
as the night loses warmth.
I've seen love die a slow death as lovers try to keep alive
against a sea of obstacles, against a roaring tide,
The lovers' hearts, the lovers' mind, they struggle in the night
Unless they choose to stay awake, love slowly dies a tragic death.

I Have Died a Thousand Deaths

I have died a thousand deaths
Loving you so completely
With every pain and rejection
You stabbed my heart and pierced my soul.
I cut my heart each night
and resurrected every morning.
Hoping you will infuse a new life in me.
My life became a continuous case
of dying and living,
Until the day it finally came…
Death.

Box

We move confined in a box
That gets smaller by the day
Today it has become a dot
Where we cannot move.

Chasm

ACing gap
   Hurt that gets deeper
  GAping hole we can no longer fill
UnSpoken, unresolved questions
DreaMs no longer the same.

The Wandering Souls

Have you ever met life's wandering souls
They're aimless and will
one day find themselves old,
Without purpose, with wornout shoes,
They are restless spirits searching for a home.
Continuously looking for something that lasts
When excitement is gone, they think love is lost.
The reality is they don't know how to love,
Love to them is a thing that is abstract.
They have not experienced what loving means,
The only love they've known is the love of self.

Storm

Dark clouds pregnant with rain
Remind me I need to take shelter.
Being wet and cold
is not a pleasant feeling.

Thank You for my Gifts

I thank you for my gifts…
You allowed me to experience sorrow
so that I can access joy.

You let me experience hurt
so I can understand my pleasure.

You made me love you more than my life
So I can love myself.

You allowed me to see injustice
So I can see what it means to be fair.

You took away my dignity
So I can regain my self-respect.

You have shown me what rejection is
So I can accept myself.

You showed me what betrayal is
So I can be honest with myself

You made me see my ugliness
So I can discover my beauty.

You told me memories means nothing
So I can appreciate my past.

You taught me to be numb
So I can learn to feel again.

You promised me nothing
So I can learn to hope.

You taught me how to hide my grief
So I can allow my tears to fall again.

You showed me how fleeting time is
So I can grasp eternity.

You ended our friendship
So I can remember I have other friends.

You never said you loved me
So I can learn to love unconditionally.

All these things I have learned from you
They are gifts from 'life',

     thank you.

At Last, Tears

I celebrate today
They flowed like rain
Cathartic, healing
Like rain, pouring.

How Do You Process Grief?

How do you process grief
when something terrible happens?
There's no other way except to access love
and forgiveness within yourself.
Nothing can beat that.
Light always defeats darkness,
Love always wins over hate.
Forgiveness triumphs over bitterness.
Seek justice but forgive.
Love overcomes.

I endure, I suffer, I give birth...

...the art of letting go

Volume II

A Woman's Hurt

A woman's love endures all things,
Suffers in silence…...
But hurt her once so painfully,
or wound her continuously……..
   Then she can take all things,
    including letting go…..

Lovers

A light so bright
the promise of warmth
a chance at life.
So sweet for a time
until it grows cold and dark.
You hurt,
accept,
understand,
move on.
A part of you dies,
But life begins again,
You live.

The Heart is a Lonely Hunter

The heart is a lonely hunter
It searches far and wide
trying to find beauty in a world that's lonely,
full of hate and dark.
It is a solitary being looking for love.
It is a lonely search,
It could last for months or years,
or a lifetime.
Sometimes the heart keeps looking
until the day it dies, but never finds,
Yet the heart goes on and never tires.
It looks for meaning in the wrong places,
leading to heartache and broken dreams…
Every heart wants love in whatever shape or form
It longs to find beauty,
and peace that the world cannot fathom…
Yes, the search is intense for the quiet truth,
the elusive love, the meaning of life.
But isn't that what life is all about?
That there is a deeper reason for all
than meets the eye
Let our hearts never tire looking
for that which is essential….
Then and only then can we find
the true meaning of life.

What is inside my Grandma's closet?

What is inside my Grandma's closet?
I know somehow it is full of secrets.
Secrets from long ago that only she knows
Quite hidden and not revealed.
She was a woman so beautiful inside and loving
She did her duties when we were young
Cooking and sewing and cleaning and washing
Never complaining whether it rains or shines.
What is inside my Grandma's closet?
One day she left it open when she went to town
I tried looking as I was curious
Never knowing what I will find.
I found an old white shawl so beautiful with lace
Used as a wrap for a bunch of old pressed flowers
With it was a letter so old and somewhat faded
The writing was smudged
as they've been wet and then dried.
The letter talked of love from a man who was gone
He sounded like someone who loved her
and yet said goodbye
He left her for something I could not understand.

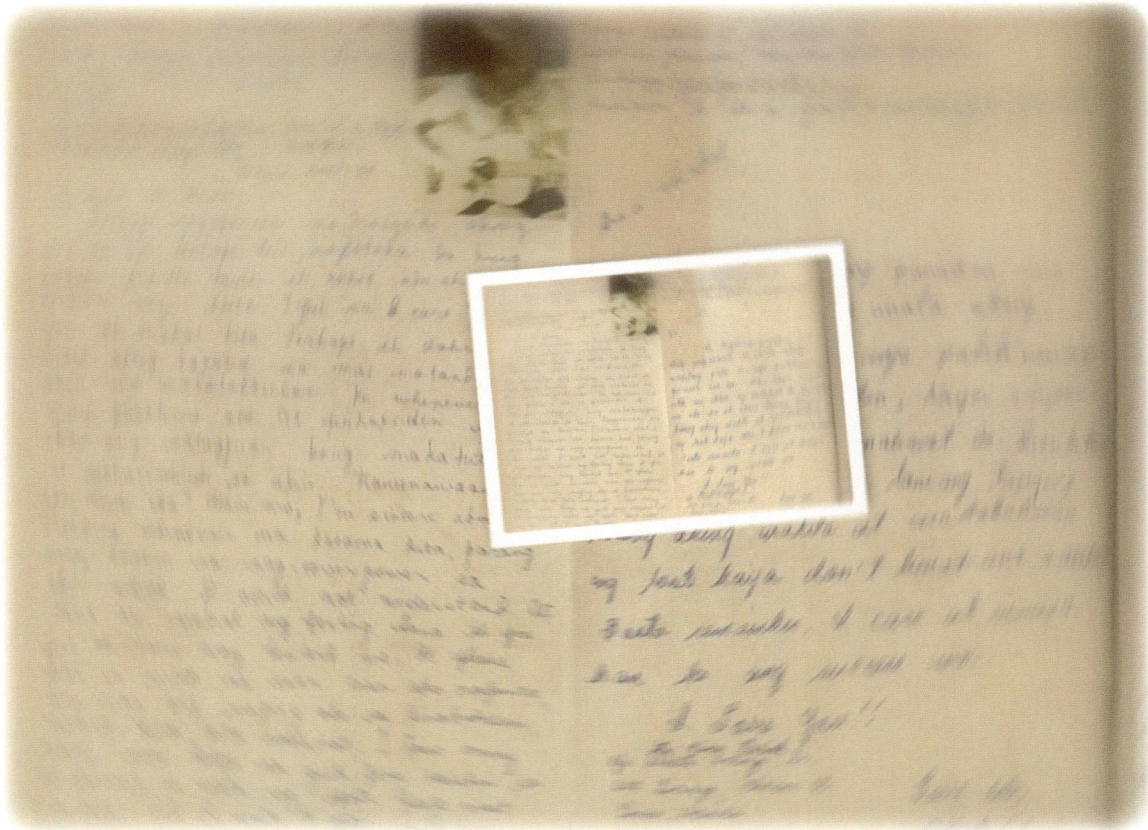

Years later Grandma died and it was then I realized
She had loved a man so deeply in her time
Loved him so much all the days of her life.
I did not know the man as he was not my Grandpa
Yet Grandma looked after Grandpa
'til the day that he died.
Never complaining, always faithfully,
She went about her sworn duty.

What is inside my Grandma's closet?
I found out the letter was faded and now I know why,
It's been wet with tears every night,
She had cried all her life always loving the man,
The one who said he loved her
and yet said goodbye.
He walked away for something
I could not understand.
I asked why would he leave
when he so loved my Grandma?
Was he weak, was he sick, was he fooling her?
Was he not free to love her?
Why did he not fight for her
when he claimed he cared?
I wanted answers but my young mind
could not grasp.

What else is inside my Grandma's closet?
She had photos of old, when she was young,
Happy, smiling and alive with this man.
Inside her closet were memories, of joy, and tears,
And dreams that she had but never came to pass.
I loved her so dearly and remember her words…
She spoke so softly before she died,
she said to me –
'Granddaughter, when you grow up,
you too will fall in love.
Promise me you will not be like me.
I suffered in silence.
I existed, but never lived.
When you find the love of your life, fight for it.
Fulfil your dreams, your heart's deepest longings.
Take hold of your destiny.
Then and only then can you be true to yourself.'

In Memoriam (for Dorina, for Corazon, my teachers in life)

I stare in sadness
thinking about you.
You inspired me to write poetry,
be creative, that it was good to love books.
You told me once.....
"S. H. E. – meaning (Significant Human Experience)
That experience allows a person to be creative,
to write from the heart."
You wrote in my highschool notebook
       "You're so young Rowena, how can you write about sadness?
        Have you experienced S. H. E. ?"
That time my young heart could not understand.
But now am older, I know.
You're so right....
I have experienced pain, sadness, life, living, grieving, loving, being loved,
being rejected, giving, letting go, yes S.H.E.....
You said "Write girl, you were born to write.".…
I finally listened to you, I guess it's too late for you to see.
You would have been happy…
I grieve, yes I grieve.…
Yet I feel so privileged that I have known you.
You have touched my life, and all of us…
Beautiful teacher, mentor, friend, inspiration, author.…

To the Children I Never Had

I see you in my dreams
I embrace you in my sadness
I long for you when I am hurting
I miss your little footsteps down the hallway.
I send you kisses and hugs
wherever, whenever you are.
…..I have loved you.

The Way of the Butterfly

I saw a butterfly today.
He kissed me on the cheek then left.
Before he went away he whispered something in my ear,
"This is a secret. I loved a flower, then left her.
She was so sad, I loved her so, but I had to go.
She cried, "I could not understand why you love me
and yet you have to go"."

I smiled at him and said "I understand.
Butterflies are meant to fly and be free."
He flew once more, I looked at him 'til he was gone.
I went my way…smiling…understanding…
Sadness aching in my heart.

'There are things we need to accept in life, no matter how painful'.

I Am as Free as the Ocean

I am as free as the ocean, as open as the sky,
I see islands of dreams in front of me,
Everything is possible within my reverie.
Dreams of fairy tales and goblins,
and lovers holding hands,
a quiet life, a peaceful world
and happy faces declaring love.
Eyes closed, I see a beautiful world.
Only the wet sand under my feet
brings me back to now.

Nocturnal

It is twilight…
Soon, I will fellowship with moon,
stars and night.
Solitude fills me as darkness comes…
I close my eyes…
I feel the pain that loneliness brings,
The silence is deafening.
Yet I bask in solitude's beauty…
It brings its own sense of comfort…
A kind of inner joy within
Like knowing one's true authentic self.
It is well with my soul….
I'm at peace within me, with the divine,
with the world, with humanity.
For a moment, the universe and me are one.

I see the moon in all her glory
(I pretend I can talk to her, asking whether we can play)
The stars twinkle like little diamonds
(I wish I can wear them on my fingers)
The clouds are like soft feathers painted on canvass
(I'd like to hold them in my hands).
I see shadows of trees' branches dancing in the wind
(I wish they were graceful men asking me to dance).
Peace,
Serenity,
Quiet repose of my soul.
I welcome the night.
I welcome its beauty.
Sleep tight, sweet dreams my dear love…
Lights out,
    good night.

Metamorphosis

The ugly worm today
is tomorrow's beautiful butterfly.

Eternal Spirit, Undying Hope

The sun never goes down
It waits patiently beyond the mountains
And after the long dark nights of sorrow
It rises again in the core of men.

My Art is my Refuge

My Art is my refuge,
I hide behind its shadow....
It allows me to be sad, to be happy,
to be anything that I can be...
It makes me one with those
who are in tears
And understand the joy
that makes others smile.......

My Art like my shadow
reflects the real me
I cannot hide from it, or run from it
It knows me, it challenges me
I cannot pretend it doesn't exist.
My Art cajoles me from complacency
It does not allow me to be passive,
or silent or thrive in mediocrity.

My Art is my refuge
when tribulation comes
My creativity flows in the face of adversity
It allows expression as
the storms of life come.

My Art is my refuge
in the face of hurt
It remains faithful like the sun everyday
It waits patiently when
I grow silent and weary
I travail, I birth, I create,
Then healing comes,
And something beautiful is born .

Changing…Loving myself, Loving others…

Finding my destiny…

Volume III

Somewhere in Time

Somewhere in time
There was a woman
Who waited and hoped and loved.
Sitting by the train station
Waiting for the man who promised
he will come back.
She never became tired,
she waited long,
Until one day she realized
she has a life of her own.
"I deserve to be loved, cared for and respected
I will search for someone, until the very end."
It was so long ago and so far away
This story that I'm telling you now.
Somewhere in time,
do you think she found someone?

From an old book I read, this was what she said-
"I am a woman racing against time
I searched far and wide for *someone.*
Thank God I found love and meaning and grace
And never lost it again to time and space…..
People say impossible, how could it be?
I say yes, it is possible to be free.
The *someone* that I found was 'me'."

Woman's true freedom comes from finding her 'Truth' and loving herself.
More than anyone, she is her very own soulmate ".

Changing

Change a blowin'
I can see from afar
Wind in my direction
Don't know what's happening,
Just go with it…
The rest will be history in no time
When you look back and say
It wasn't too bad after all,
The storm passes, the pain is gone,
You realize there's strength within you,
Untapped and dormant but alive and real.
You have given birth to a new self, a new freedom
that is free and unencumbered,
No more fear of losing someone
No baggage, no injustice,
No tears, no hurt.
I am a woman wanting change,
wanting my life back as there's lots to do.
Out there, there's a lot of pain
I can do something
From the valley of tears, I hear crying, people dying
I can't stand not doing…
Listening, helping, that's my destiny,
I can't deny, I can't resist
I was born to do it, else there is no rest!

Change is knocking, can you hear what I'm hearin'?
I can hear the 'Deep' callin'
I can hear 'Spirit' sayin',
"Channel your energy to those who are hurting.
You were born for such a time,
All things are new, the old has passed."
Change a-comin'
Like waves a-rollin'
Can you hear the gentle whisper?
Just go with it.
To be free and without burden
Is bliss, is joy, is rest.
Have a look at me now,
See the smile on my lips,
The peace I have within my heart,
The people are callin'
That is my life now,
No time for selfish desires
And dreams that will never rhyme.
'Spirit' says 'Yield',
Yes, I come,
I am in a hurry,
Life is too short to think a lot about myself…
It is not about me, it is not about me.
…..That is my most important change.

Moon, Sun

I am moon,
you are sun
Never the two shall meet.
Working together,
Same goal, same dream
but at a distance.
Each gives light to a
dark and dying world.

When I Look into your Eyes

When I look into your eyes
I see your soul smile at me,
The moon and stars dance
to celebrate our friendship.

Why me, my sweetheart?

You know I am no pin-up girl, vital stats quite ordinary
I fumble and am clumsy
Not the best cook in the kitchen either;
Driving is not my cup of tea ,
and street direction am hopeless in.
I giggle and smile too much
Cry at the most silly things,
Always teary-eyed, mushy, a softie
Known to dance non-stop crazy.
I wear quirky clothes that seldom match
Throw me a ball, I may not catch.
 I don't pretend am a vamp in bikini…
And oh dear, sexy high-heels are not for me.
So why me, my sweetheart?
I guess I don't seem like the best girl around.
But I have love though,
Lots and lots of it,
and smiles that never run out for you.
I love people, love life,
I don't pretend,
I am real, unsophisticated in fact,
But more than anything, I believe in you.
I'm your number one cheerleader, you might say,
But sweetheart, I guess you knew that anyway.

An Ode to Friendship

Isn't it that I just talk and she listens?
No earth-shaking words of wisdom
Just a nod, a knowing look,
a heart that understands.
Sometimes it is just silence….
But it's enough to make me feel better.
She can cry when am sad
She's happy when I am
She knows my pain and joy….
Always proud of me
whilst she knows
my warts and imperfections.
That's friendship.
I glow in its warmth…
I bathe in its beauty.

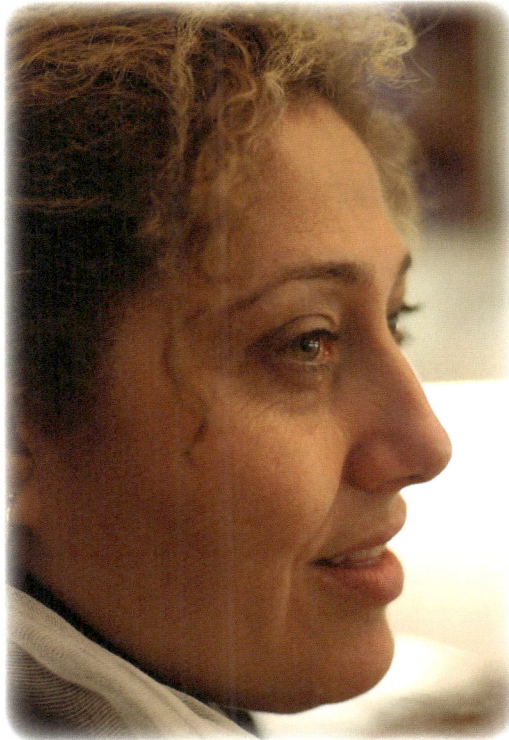

Kindred Spirits

Without telling me your pain
I feel them
I write and you understand
You shake my roots sometimes
Like a storm to a tree
With fury and anger
Moving me until I shiver.
You love me in rhyme and words
the way the pen loves delicate paper
It puts its mark gently
caressing , touching through graceful letters.
Kissing with passion, loving in words.
I embrace you now in absence,
I feel your presence.

There is no distance between us,
A different love we share
Of soul and spirit beyond the flesh and time;
Deeper,
Tolerant,
Kind,
Patient,
Silent,
Gentle,
Giving,
Selfless.

You know my pain, my thoughts, my joy,
Understand my unspoken self deep inside my being,
It is a different place,
yes, a different world where we meet.

Building Bridges

I want to build a bridge
between you and me,
With all my strength
I will reach out and touch you.
Two people connected so deeply
cannot be strangers forever,
Yesterday's bitterness
can be erased by time,
by love, and understanding.
In some distant future,
when you are down and lonely,
You will find a friend
waiting at the other end,
It will be me.

Gifts are Not Always about Happiness

I knew a woman who was in love.
Her face was haggard.
She had wrinkles, lines and bony hands.
She visited the seashore whenever she can
Reminiscing the love of her life.
She would cry, she knew tears
She experienced love, and loved with all her heart.

I met a man who once loved a girl.
His sight was failing,
His clothes were tattered and old,
Slept and stayed in the park all days of the year.
But he had a smile, a far away gaze,
He had stars in his eyes.
He experienced love, and loved with all his heart.

Let me ask you a question,
are they not the luckiest souls

If I were the President

If I were the President
Most days will be holidays
The President's House will host fun rides in tandem
A red rose will be the country's emblem.
Surnames will be women's after two have joined
Kids will be agenda in meetings of the boards.
Guns will burst with beautiful flowers
And tanks will have white scarves with laces.
Food will reach every starving mouth
Just as someone's Divine hand has planned.
You may say I am a dreamer
And yes I guess I am,
But won't it be a better world
Compared to what we have?

Grace and Beauty at Twilight

How graceful, how beautiful can a creature be?
Such slender neck, what exquisite form,
So lovely to behold.
She mesmerizes, she exudes magic
At twilight time.
She taught me a profound truth that night:

'A woman's beauty is never forced, it is innate. It comes from grace inside.
People feel it rather than see it; and when they do, joy is experienced'.

Aung San Suu Kyi : A Tribute to a Beautiful Woman

A woman's beauty is a mystery,
It makes the morning bright when she smiles,
A tense night calm with her quiet repose,
It is like the moonbeam that
gives warmth on a cold dark night,
A white flower that casts a lovely fragrance.
A woman's beauty can be seen in her eyes
They show kindness when children are hurting
They shed tears to bond with those of broken hearts.
In her is compassion, mercy and great love
Not just for herself but for her country, her people,
the oppressed, the hungry and the weak.
And when this love is translated into action,
Showing strength and fighting for justice
Speaking 'truth' in a world full of sham and false values
Declaring war to have a bright future for mankind,
That is when she is most beautiful.

Gaze

Yes, there is sadness,
it is dark outside.
but i see beyond the war, hatred,
devastation and poverty.
I see a future of hope, peace,
love and prosperity.
you see, I am Woman.

Time and the Rhythm of Life

Time is like soldiers marching on to war
They move on in earnest, without looking back.
Leaving mothers, homeland, friends and loved ones
No respect for season, whether cold or warm.

'Time waits for no one', so my grandpa says,
All regrets, or remorse, they are all from the past.
'Look forward, my grandchild, that's all you can do,
Nothing lasts forever,
You just have to push through.'

Looking back at my life
Lots of joy, lots of pain,
Loved ones from the past
I wonder how they've been?

Friends gained, friends lost
Memories shared from the past,
They bring a smile to my lips,
How I wish they would last.

Innocence lost, knowledge gained
I wonder which is better,
Love the things I have learned
But maybe slept more soundly when
I didn't know what loving was,
or losing dreams, a story's end,
All I know was I played then
And at eight I was in bed.

All the same no regret,
Time marches on,
Just the same I can't exchange
what I had in life 'til the end.

Time is an enemy, an ally,
A concept that's man-made
As for me I'd like to think
Time is still a faithful friend.

'There is a rhythm and cycle of life and death that keeps going for all beings,
All we can do is flow gracefully and enjoy the dance of the moment'.

Free!!!

I am a bird in flight
I am the open and boundless sea
I am the wind blowing sounds of liberty
I am the sun radiating warmth in all its glory
I am the moon providing solace at night
I am the stars inspiring mortals to aim high
I am poetry flowing freely with rhythm
I am a woman dancing to music without care
I am a man moving on to realize dreams
I am a child sleeping soundly at night
I am a *people* liberated from oppression,
believing in themselves,
rebuilding lives,
reclaiming rights they have,
to be free from fear and pursue happiness.
I am the ability to express love,
My name is Freedom
I am life itself…
Without me, what is life?

The lips of a woman must speak the truth

The lips of a woman must speak the truth
Proclaim beauty in whatever form
Speak on behalf of the defenseless
and the oppressed
Lift people's spirit,
Express compassion
Shake complacency
And declare love for humanity.
Out of the woman's mouth,
there could be redemption…

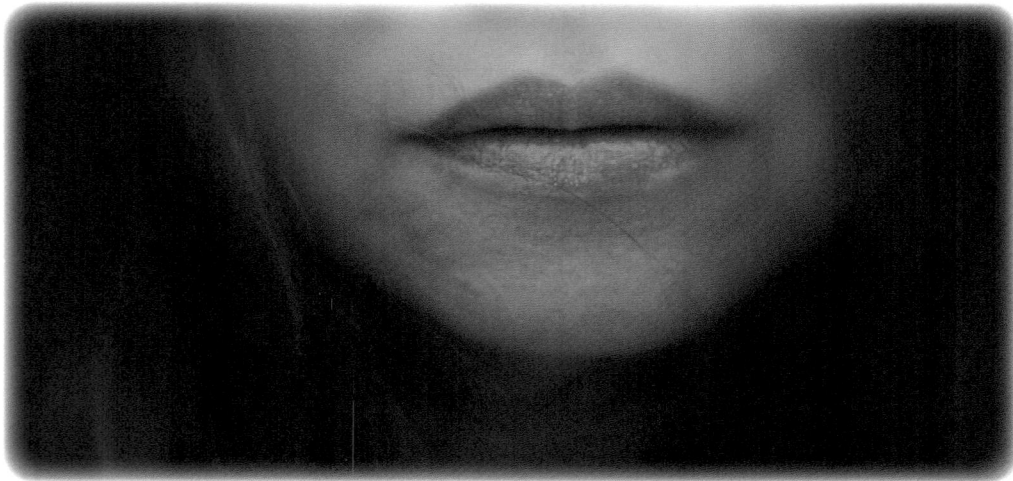

The Forsaken Muse Finds Herself

Volume IV

Man and Woman Together

Woman and Man hand in hand,
Honouring each other's place in love, in peace,
in wisdom and what each one can contribute.
Growing in consciousness, in awareness, both of them,
Recognizing each other and the role each one plays
to make society a better place to live in.
Man respecting woman as an equal, with her brain, her grace,
her talent, her contribution to society.
He has to see her inner beauty, essence and points of view.
Man helps a woman find herself, the same way a woman helps a man.

Woman Finding Herself

Woman should honour herself as a woman.

Have self-respect, and not allow herself to be portrayed lowly.

There won't be 'robot-like dolls', 'nude angels', dumb secretaries, women in chains, portrayed kissing snakes, wallowing in mud, posing in the most degrading of circumstances if we don't allow ourselves to be portrayed as such.

This is a hard battle, especially for our younger kind, and this is why the more mature of us have a mandate to be responsible role models.

We need to project what women truly are in society, that majority of us are more than what we see in ads, images, movies, and tv. Just like our *Forsaken Muse*, we need to understand that we are all *Muses* to the world, that we inspire creativity, hope, and life in a world that is growing more and more cynical. That we are not so forsaken or forgotten after all, whatever our age, our looks or circumstances are, and that we can still contribute to the well-being of the younger ones, or the weaker ones amongst us.

We feed the weak, the young, the hungry, and provide solace to those who need help.

We love, we care, we think, we speak, we are body and soul, we help humanity.

We are mothers, teachers, nurses, sisters, grandmothers, students, health workers, doctors, engineers, helpers, care workers, volunteers for those in need, a comfort for those who are hurting…We have spirit, spunk, we are beautiful in our own special way, each one of us.

A new consciousness, a new awareness of our own power, ability, and even weaknesses should come. This is strength in itself.

Finally, we as women (young and old), need to find ourselves, come of age by ourselves, and come to a realization of our purposes in the world in which we live in, and know who we truly are. We should find our true selves and essence alone, as an individual and then corporately. Then and only then can freedom and liberation come.

"How beautiful can a woman be? No one can be more beautiful than a woman who has loved her country and people more than her own self, who has suffered unselfishly to pursue happiness and freedom for all. After years of suffering, oppression and abuse, she comes out older yet full of wisdom, lines on her eyes and face that can't hide her inner beauty and character, a frail figure that is more attractive than the media stereotypes of 'allure', a woman whose love of humanity, freedom and truth has caused her to remain resolute. They can kill her body, but not her spirit."

Dedicated to women all over the world at
various points in time who have been
imprisoned, displaced, or even
killed for their love of country, their God, their
beliefs and their people.

With Thanks and Love

'We meet people everyday. But there are some who touch our lives in a deeper way, as if we've known them all our lives. We may not see them everyday, or for years and years, but we feel the same love, as if they have not left us. Real friendship is beyond time and space.'

Writing a book of poetry is a dream that I've had since I was a little girl. I still can't believe that I have done it. And I have to say, this would not have been possible if it were not for the love, support, faith, encouragement, loving reminders, and advice that my family, friends, colleagues, teachers, and fellow artists have given me. The Forsaken Muse, a Woman's Journey from Sorrow to Hope would have been a beautiful but impossible dream for me without these people around me.

With faith, I acknowledge a 'Divine' presence within my life that has not let me rest within myself until I give a message that I need to send out as an artist and as a woman. It seems He has not given me any choice but to 'birth' this out.

I thank with affection my family who has put up with my 'quirky' behaviour (at times), timetable, and 'poet moments' as I was writing, especially when deadline was near. I think the boys deserve a special mention: Raoul, my husband, and my sons Michael, Daniel and Eldie (an adorable golden retriever who stayed beside me in the long nights before the deadline; he is like a 'son' too).

I dedicate this to many girlfriends in various parts of the world who I love, adore and share 'soul feeding' time with, online or face to face when we meet on holidays or international work assignments or around Sydney. I send you blessings and kisses; you are my inspiration for writing this book. Special mention goes to Leanne Magoulias who has stuck by me through my best and worst times, and believed in me whatever happens, to Ros o' Brien, a loving work colleague, to Flordeliza Martiniano Bruinink who has long provided support and encouragement, to Elsa, Nitz, Graciela C, Virgie Lynn, Dahlee A, Leilani, Renelita, Lita, Carmi, Kitt, Olive, Susan, Marilyn, Emma, Lucille and all my girl batchmates from highschool, my BFF's from uni days Matet, Gina, Chayong, Ann, Mona, Ces Z, Didit, Manang Susan D, Judy G, Cynthia , Marge, Chona S, Ophelia B, Irynn A and others, my other lovely girlfriends Fiona T, Gabby, Jennifer C, Charmaine, June W, Louise, Karina C & Aliyah, Digna, Net V, Flor R, and Noemi . My girlfriends include my sisters Rosanna, Riza and Kelly.. I'd like to mention too my support crew from Authorhouse: Portia, John, Audrey, Joe Burns, Erin W and Jonah; without them, this book will not have gone to production in time for the NY exhibit. Special dedication as well to the Red Bubble community, a community of artists online that I am a part of. I have learned so much from fellow artists in this great site.

I dedicate this too to a few male friends who have loved me like a sister and have faith in what I can do- Russell Ives, Marcelino Bernardo, Alex Pascua, Tom Maceda, Allan Mauricio, Paeng Santos, Niranjan Deodhar, Leon Fertman, Pepito Cabigas, Dante Lomibao, Glenn Altern, Dheeraj Marcus and Jonathan Hartland, a friend who reminded me that I still have the 'gift' to write poetry, and with whom I did collaborations in photography to produce some beautiful images.

I won't be the woman that I am today if not for my beautiful Mama and my loving Papa (I call him Tata) who treated me like a lady all my life and believed in me even when I was a little girl. I remember too my Grandma Irinea, my inspiration in the poem 'What is inside my Grandma's Closet?' She is long gone but I remember her always and her lessons.

To my brothers and sisters at MCF, I thank you for providing a loving spiritual home to us. Special mention to some ladies: Sue M & Sue S, Sandra, Greta, Heather, Sandi K, Alison, Shannon K, Shannon T, Jaz, Karina, Marilyn, Peggy, and all the other women from MCF.

To the men who have been a part of me at various times in my life, I thank you too. Without you, I would not have the experience, insight and inspiration for some of my poetry. I thank you for your gifts of 'learning.'

My love and thanks go to my kindred spirit, the beloved Australian poet NANUSHKA, my dear Nan, who has kindly reviewed my materials out of love and has given me the confidence to realize my dreams. She is such a great encouragement to me. She has provided her commentary for my book so generously. We connected by accident which I believe is 'Divine-ordained'.

This book is also written to keep alive the memory of my cousin, Dr Gerry Ortega, a staunch environmentalist and wildlife veterinarian who died not so long ago because of his tireless work to protect the environment of the beautiful islands of Palawan. A number of the book's images were taken from Palawan, the Last Ecological Frontier of the Philippines. I will always be proud that I'm your cousin Gerry.

With all my love and gratitude, this book is for all of you who have been a part of me, even if I have not mentioned your name. I hope it speaks to you and provides you with some answers to life.

Special credits:

Raoul Isidro – for most photographs and art work and the creative design of my concept for the front and back cover.
Zorica Purlija – photography of images (The Show is Over, If I Were The President and Tragic Love)
Carol Ritchie – photography of image (Acknowledgement Page)
David Miller – photography of image (Gaze)
Rowena Isidro – photography of images (Grace And Beauty At Twilight, Kiss, When I Look into your Eyes, Lovers, Lips of an Artist, Grandma's Closet, Nocturnal, An Ode to Friendship, The Way of the Butterfly)
Stevie-Lee DeFranciscis– model (When I Look Into Your Eyes)
Aliyah Palu – model (Kiss, The Way of the Butterfly)
Daniel Isidro – model (Kiss)
Palawan, Philippines – for its beautiful islands, sea and shoreline in some of the images
Sydney, Australia – wonderful city, lovely backdrop for many images
Architectural Perspectives Australia - for book cover design and graphic arts services

For Further Information

ROWENA ISIDRO would love to hear from you as you embark on your own personal journey as a woman, just like 'The Forsaken Woman' in the book. If you are interested in additional reading materials, resources and Rowena's forthcoming books, book launches and seminars, please contact her on the following email, mailing address and/or Facebook account. Rowena's seminars on 'A Woman's Journey to Self-discovery' includes materials from various poems, poetic proses and essays which are laden with philosophical and spiritual insights.

rowena.isidro@bigpond.com
or

PO Box 11
Mascot
NSW
Australia 2020
or

Facebook Account: The Forsaken Muse, A Woman's Journey From Sorrow To Hope – Book of Poetry

Every woman has a story of survival. They sometimes stumble, but they rise up to redeem themselves for the sake of loved ones, or even for their own dignity. They could be crushed, shaken for awhile but never defeated. They have their scars and wounds, but they are survivors, they are victorious and prevail at the end.

About the Author

Rowena Isidro has been writing poetry since she was a young girl. People who have read her work comment that her writing takes them to another world. Her writing is a contradiction: childlike, easy to read, simple, yet can be surreal, romantic, passionate, dreamy and practical. Her work shows her maturity as a woman, her wisdom and philosophy in life. She naturally loves people, engaging in social service, supporting women issues and mentoring other people. Rowena is a writer, an activist, a philosopher, an engineer, a poet, a mother, sometimes a part-time model, a student photographer, a fashion designer/stylist and an IT consultant. She lives in Sydney with her boys and a much-loved golden retriever. She is a busy woman, but always has time to listen to people. She has a ready smile for everyone, quite transparent and bares her soul so easily. The best description for her is 'She is a woman, but always a child at heart'. She is a fascinating study in contradiction.

CPSIA information can be obtained
at www.ICGtesting.com
2365LVUK00002B